Yellow Umbrella Books are published by Capstone Press
151 Good Counsel Drive, P.O. Box 669, Mankato, Minnesota 56002
http://www.capstone-press.com

Library of Congress Cataloging-in-Publication Data
Curry, Don L.
How things move/by Don L. Curry.
p. cm.
Includes index.
ISBN 0-7368-0724-1
1. Force and energy—Juvenile literature. [1. Force and energy.] I. Title.
QC73.4 .C87   2001
531'.6—dc21   330530   00-036473

Summary: Explains the concept of push and pull movement, using many examples.

Editorial Credits:
Susan Evento, Managing Editor/Product Development; Elizabeth Jaffe, Senior Editor;
    Jessica Maldonado, Designer; Kimberly Danger and Heidi Schoof, Photo Researchers

Photo Credits:
Cover: Jeffry W. Myers/Pictor; Title Page: John Terence Turner/FPG International LLC; Page 2:
Index Stock Imagery; Page 3: Bob Daemmrich/Pictor; Page 4: John Terence Turner/FPG
International LLC (left), Adamsmith/FPG International LLC (right); Page 5: Transparencies,
Inc./Robert Cavin, Bob Daemmrich/Pictor (inset); Page 6: Jim Cummins/FPG International
LLC (left), Richard Price/FPG International LLC (right); Page 7: Photophile/Mark E. Gibson
(left), International Stock/R. Tesa (right); Page 8: Unicorn Stock Photos/Aneal Vohra (left),
International Stock/Scott Barrow (right); Page 9: Index Stock Imagery (left), Photo
Network/Fabricius-Taylor (right); Page 10: Pictor; Page 11: Photo Network/Dennis Junor; Page
12: Pictor; Page 13: VCG/FPG International LLC; Page 14: Brian Parker/TOM STACK &
ASSOCIATES; Page 15: International Stock/Mitch Diamond; Page 16: Llewellyn/Pictor

1 2 3 4 5 6 06 05 04 03 02 01

How Things Move

by Don L. Curry

Consulting Editor: Gail Saunders-Smith, Ph.D.
Consultants: Claudine Jellison and
Patricia Williams, Reading Recovery Teachers
Content Consultant: Vivian O'Dell, Staff Scientist,
Fermi National Accelerator Lab

Yellow Umbrella Books

an imprint of Capstone Press
Mankato, Minnesota

We push or pull things
to make them move.

We push on the pedals
of a bike.
We push away with one foot
and then the other to skate.

We push the oars
against the water
to row a boat.
We push a bat
to hit a ball.

We pull the handle
of a wagon.
We pull the rope of a sled.

We pull an apple
from a tree.
We pull a brush
through our hair.

We sometimes use both pushes and pulls to move things. We push a rolling pin across dough, and then we pull it back.

Someone may pull us back and then push us forward on a swing. The harder they pull and push, the higher and faster we will go.

When we play a violin,
we push and pull the bow
across the strings.
The pushes and pulls
make the strings move.
This movement makes sound.

Pushes and pulls make things move in different ways.

Things move back and forth.

Things move up and down.

Things move
around and around.

Things even move in a zigzag.

Things sometimes move fast.

Things sometimes move slow.

Things move many ways
when we push or pull them.

Words to Know/Index

brush—to smooth hair with a brush; a brush is a tool with bristles and a handle; page 7

dough—a sticky mix used to prepare baked goods; page 8

forth—forward; something may move back and forth; this means it moves from side to side or backward and forward; page 11

movement—the act of changing position from place to place; page 10

pedal—a lever that works when a foot pushes on it; bicycles and cars have pedals; page 4

rolling pin—a tube-shaped kitchen tool used to flatten dough; page 8

skate—to move along on skates; a skate is a shoe with wheels or a blade on the bottom; page 4

violin—a musical instrument with four strings, played with a bow; page 10

wagon—a cart with four wheels and a long handle; page 6

zigzag—a line that moves quickly in short, sharp turns from side to side; page 14

Word Count: 212
Early-Intervention Levels: 9–12